Chapter 1. Women's Taken a hold of the glory that were

Created in them.
This Book Dedicate to my Niece's Nephew Sadavina Cannon and Alice Cannon Jericho, Alice Davis Le- Willie Davis On the behave of their First Cousin Angelo T Uscanga Wimbush and, Jamar E Uscanga Wimbush

http://propheticministry.webs.com-
YouTube
sharon481000

Pursue
Founding Their Life's missing Piece's

Women's Taken a Hold to the Glory that were created in them Women's

No More Tears ♪♪ Tear's
(Issue's (Honey)

The Missing Piece's

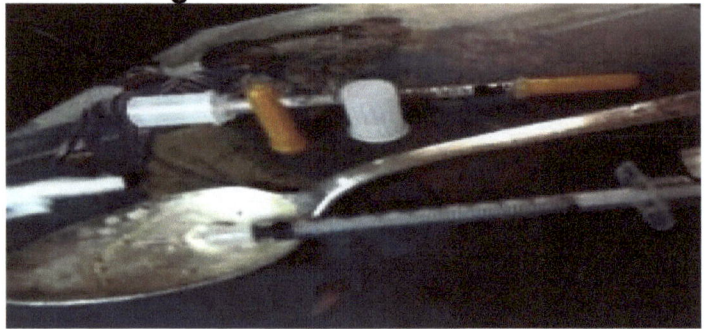

Broken Hearted

Fighting the Battler alone

Women's First Let me start "by telling you how beautifully you are; on the inside.

This must be a time that is needed to take a rest from the other world...Issue" No Food in the home;

struggle over the man I Love: changing really travel from a further away –

Fighting the battler alone we must understand that feeling of the rebirth against God Word…. Move out of self-trap inside a door that can't be. Heart broken Neck tie Rumor's the go Trying to new feeling bring on a broke through Meeting surrounding the rap path of the haulage H. One in a Life time do we make money do we show Patient.

1. Answer to this is that if; I call a name will it hurt. The Answer is (Issue)
2. Trying to pull a strong hold from away from other people: Just to see the Earth and, the fulfill. The Answer is (Missing Piece's)
3. Take a chance's over the world and, Letting Satan in. The Answer (fighting the battler along).

Broken Hearted

Face the Trail Time asking myself;" what

Must I do? Seeing Simon the one of the

Apostle Name as to remember were Peter

Too---- I knew this man of God---- Women's A

Broken Hearted is a Reminder of the dictator That we receive---- Peter Sir Name Simon

Were a Fisherman of God; A Broken hearted

Come from an evil man not one that are fish

Man for the Lord ----- Lady's don't you know

That you can hurt your spouse you're mate-

And, receive A Broken Hearted,,,

Think for a minute what a broken hearted is
Like taken a
Flower break it into pieces and,

Meditate on this. The heart in the body catch
Up with the mind" So that the hearts pull in
Trouble from people Lie's and, this hurt the
Mind and, break the heart.

*Broken Hearted Cry Aloud take this heart is
broken into pain the feeling around the
heart" make the difference 'in doing for the
person the worth is over making a change….
One time women gave them self to words
that hurt them.*

*The Heart breaks no good out of Life. One's
say truthing in my feeling. The heart of the
Lost is another heart are you…? One that
been Hurt Broken Hearted before saying for*

example I got my heart hurt in a relationship,,, The Step's to helping building better.

Relationship

STEP: ONE Broken Hearted:

Taken a step out of Fear… with your relationship setting up time to fellowship and, making the time right to talk don't talk to a good relationship with bad news about other that have hurt: you if they don't ask: why is this sometime it DE strike you from remaining in a good relationship and this kill's the person Attitude from being good taken the mind into been bad--- Think toward one enough. One reason your hearts are broken ---Because it cost use trouble in our relationship with God… And, this hurt the Mind and, the body of Christ.

The Next Step to helping a relationship that been in a broken hearted is finding time to ask question from an relationship: About how not to and when to talking about how I shouldn't hurt each other when is it going to stop always catch your mate in a good move.
When talking about something that happen in your relationship this will help your relationship to see each other wrong doing and, helping them

believe that you are somebody. That is worth something.

ISSUE"S That Marriage are not; in a Relationship sharing the bed together with other money issue-------------------------------Following Short---------Trying to be the pace "Nursing the cost act on Faith " Helping is there never be afraid to share in your marriage are relationship you're deep's feeling and, secret's

Issue's--- Marriage help you to not SEX in the relationship it bring on relationship: Studying what you see other go through secretly wanting help, you're issue's how I know; follow them around are ask a friend about their issues and, Look at you and, you're issue do it help are brings's on more and more "more problems into your relationship.
Set a cup on the table turn it over put it back down on the table what do you see in it... One issue to another putting together a puzzle... Broken but not destroy----

Chapter 2.

Issue Cancel:

OUT in a relationship---- The for barren of Lust the eyes of fire that seeing pillow by night----Scared out of it hate on the Line talking to much Issue that relationship can't handle put denier's Pillow talk Jealous out to destroy, you ---- can I see me in all of This Help Help Me to Understand.

ISSUES Cancel:

In a Marriage to the believer: No cheating when one's fall into temptation SKY is purple Letter's your Red becoming looking blue this my first Mistake say all the time not going to make the same mistake anymore---- Issues in a marriage please in a marriage please cancel out Sex in another bed can you see the undefiled of the hell raising over nothing keeping it real " Fear has brought on the power to cast out fear I got to stop Sin Death Lay at the door--- You are (A) Unbeliever--- When you pick up SIN

Issues can handle your God will--- Empower turn on the LIGHT OF Jesus Christ.

The purpose of the missing pieces----
Are you in deniers of your feel's
Lady's has this been a issue for a
while--- The purpose of the Missing
piece's is denying the Glory of God---
He's right now you're everything… But
the missing piece's we do need God;
word when something is missing in
your Life turn to you; say Iam still
here.

MISSING PIECE'S

My Love one die when I were 5 year old and, I
can't seem to conquer the missing piece's
this woman put into my Life.''' Now she is die
and she grow me up now I'm 25 year old I
really miss her I really do but there is still
something missing. The Missing pieces are
you lack of Faith. What this mean that you
have understanding of God and, who God is
but do I have enough power and, hope for
tomorrow. When I truth God for his
Knowledge on how to receive a blessing how
do I go by it I can't look at a window and truth
that I can see out of it but when I pray to God
for a blessing this is how; I looked at it hope
that my praying to God will give me what I
prayed for if I believe in what I pray about.

MISSING PIECE'S

In this page will help you discover why I always sometime forget where. I Put things around the house like my keys my . purse my ring-ETC—that doesn't mean that you are losing it but the pieces are not coming together---- REACH the missing of this doing is understanding that at my busy point and, time of the day. I May not understand what is going on but I know that something is missing and, this help me to see that my mind; is not bad it just a test of my Faith that my day has a missing piece.

Fighting the batter alone:

Have you ever being around the places that you had no idea of where you were going…. This is an example of fighting the battler--- alone--- Learning on what you see may affect you personally later on wee wheeze whoa" I like this saying alone if I fight for what belong to me will I soon Remember the missing piece's --- I hate when

PEOPLE LIE on each other this put a puzzle in your mind that you don't fit in"

You are fighting the battler alone—
Really nothing to lose' but we have to
gain winner but not losing I'm here
alone and, waiting on this bus I can
emerge what might be going on at
home fighting the battler alone getting
a phone call at 5P.M in the day time to
some bad news want stop you from
getting bless alone. We ask for this
one trouble came but you are Left
alone to fight the battler alone----

Jerry can stop on the Freeway Lisa
came alone ask Jerry to help him he
left his Jake at home Lisa car stop and,
gave out of gas now both of these people are
broken down on the freeway.

Lisa call a Friend to help come Jerry know he
needed the Jake and, Lisa need gas;"
fighting the battler alone-----

                    This is a scripture to
help you" you fight your battler day after day.

Psalm 119 Verse 1
The Word is a Lamp unto my Feet, and a light
unto my path.

Chapter 3

NO MORE TEAR'S.

Anit you glad about God word----- In the best's days to come no, no no ----- More Tear's no more slave you heard the story…. But the day of No More Tears can people believe that; if someone hurt them they will cry. The no More Tear's story is true this is not a play--- We can last if we don't fast' Fasting help people to stay alive in the word… What this means no more Tear's woman don't you hurt for nothing—I don't want to see you hurt your spiritual life is a life that a person really can't see but you have to stay force the pain is tear's but the hurt fell's you if you can't handle the pain --

- God want to dread up you're Tears and bring about a charge in your Life no Tear's say you heard the story about a home broken from substance abuse are a place that took you to never land hate want limit the cost of hurt are pain when it comes down to the truth.

Thank you note---- As well as given thanks to God for everything that he has done for you make it ready an, ready-made really.

1. Knowing the true facts
2. Giving Honor
3. Ask yourself a question
4. Telling it like it is never
5. The issue will not find you know--
   -
6. The no more Tears situation is a After party why we hurt "because we see other prosperous over Victory gaining power.

How can I do this reading God word daily meditation on god Word? I find a card on day beside the ride and, it read to me isn't this a story of peace it read

at the end if you every had the end if
you every had a Tear drop out your
eye and, you visualize that you were
left to hurt then give it to Jesus the
                    Answer to you would
be no more Tears planning a trip to the
Ocean Sea crying out Loud the answer
isn't alone giving me a short story
fighting the battler alone….. I gain over my
batter and this gave me power and, the
victory over my.

                         TEAR; S
Fear, Anger; Sadness" worrying; and
Stopping---- blindness, confession
confession, confusion confession,
confuse----- blameiness, Hurting---
Power on Darkness--- Word
Transfigure and do and denial.

The Answer to all of this is No
                    MORE TEAR'S
Conquer Power this day and, hour
Tear's that don't fit in; Tears of peace
the missing peace are you at lost why

the tears of lonely or the Tears of hurt fear depression in despair never finding time to rehearsal time and patient can some help me to stay save hand working power is needed to create the since of human.

To keep the Tears from rolling... No More Tears is the answers at Jesus Feet; the vision feet is much more extra Cost and, the handle of making the understanding the answering can you vision making the word come a Live--- see the information is truthed to you--- You can see that God is awesome and, his glory is very powerfully making me believe and, be like Jesus.

The Founding of their Life is more interest. "How can:" I denied God --- He has the answer to all problems. No More Tears; There is a story to this all can you believe that him he made it really with God.

Answer to your question that we ask is true.... Judgment are really and, satisfy answer--- Do You Know God don't want no more Tear's do you remember the day of Death for Christ on the cross how they swap him and, he didn't cry he barren the pain---- there a saying that Jesus he bared the pain on the cross so that you would be bless heal and, not curse be and, see another Life.

Women's Taken belong over the "To countless Pain…. How do I feel sometimes have you tried to count the time. Haley how much time does you spend with God a day no circumstance to what we do the to count less Pain…. What are you waiting on my promise belong to God.
This is your answer to your question this countless pain never extra to you women; why can't we step out to and

past Tenth  you
see this Picture Tears is not the worthy
but it's a blessing to cry tears. The
Bible says they that cry in tears shall
reap in joy Ps 126 verse 5…. Over to
the to count Less Pain how do we
explain to the answer that singing the
Psalm of Praise will deliver you''' you
got Pg. 27 to know this as the
countless Pain bring in hurt from the
dictation of the rapt her of the glory
that are created in you this woman has
got what it take to come in line with the
promise of God something is just at
the Line to see this.

Jesus read this to his disciples, he gave them power against unclean spirits, to cast them out, and to heal all manner of sickness and all manner of disease. Countless Pain Winning the Victory: The victory over the battle has already been won.....

Women's taken belong over the to countless Pain... Moving away from hurt and, disguise of problem's that are not bring them to an End---- Winning the VICTORY IN JESUS NAME

Women's taken a hold of the glory that were created in them most of all in the midst of this saying: God made a woman in the image of Man one hundred percent man and, Woman were created out of God to stir up the Atmosphere on the inside.

The Glory helps me to see the shadier of Faith

Walking in the midst of a storm---- taken a hold of the Glory that God got out of the children of Israel Life when they; were trap in the RED SEA this getting the Glory that God bought them over on the other side of the Red Sea from other side of the Red Sea from a very anger and mad man the Pharaohs HELP One's crying the wildness bring forth Fruit;; God got the Glory out of the children Israeli Life's that he would protect them for the rest of their Life from trouble raptor and the rapt her of God... Hallelujahs are serving.

I take a hold of my problems alone without God want help you defend the needs of the problem. Women have taken a hold of the creation that was born in them holds the Glory that God got out of your problems. One reason a story never in a question because answer can be answer until a question is ask Women's, In Christ take over territory problem's.. Do you believe that power give you this control say we kill we murder we tarry down but; honestly are we together to all this. Territory attaches places one to another... Chance to stop chance stop get help chance to make away chance to deliver through the word a chance to find time in understanding people of territory's attach God gave you power over the trouble in the world today that territory problem would become under the circumstance of the Holy Ghost.

Your problem's can be God unless you become Holy this brings on holy trinity of the Holy Ghost. Women's that are in Christ know a problem of territory's--- We Face Tomorrow another world another Trail another age and, atmosphere an, another becoming Holy is the Lamb of God.

Women's Taken belonging over the rapt her that was created in Women 'God founding of their Life's Study what you read about…

I learn that founding of the Life's of a Woman

Mean's that I understand The Power of Faith that were created in me and,

God will; God is righteous until the end of you're

LIFE…..

The Raptor that in me is how I'll created… The power and, how I use it "I never thought that God could use me into the work that I do for him; some what I find in me were Trouble now I'll trouble free. The rapt her in me Freeness from the world I'm free from all evil this raptor that were created in me from God; "didn't bring in confusion but brought into me the Holy Spirit I use my rapt her as a War for the devil. The Rapter that God created in me were to bring on power to throw out the man power….. Women's Taken belong over the two and the rapt her that were created in women's of God.

The Women's Empowering Fear Book

Created this Novel Book to really seriously explain you're problems more and, you're problems more and, more to you to understand that women cast out fear to bring in God Love.

Perfect Love cast out all Fear in God. The Women's Empowering Fear mean's just what it say to you; why do we lose so much insight when out in the cross road with other one's say they don't know but ask you're self this question to see if you can really get through to an answer ."My issue is never at changeable if I don't get some help from the Lord: That's why women's taken belong over the two and the Raptor that were created in women's you can found the Life that want in you if you can believe it believe it shall come to pass.

Women how you can conquer the devil power can you give you're on answer; on

The Next Page.

Women Empowering Fear to believe from reading this book. God really love what you do when you see what God do for you.

The incredible of the doing is great and, mighty with God. The Word of God can be precious in the (EYE Sight). OF Thee Lord talking wrong is wrong with God. Doing for the Lord is right in the Eyesight of the Great I I'm The Blessing of the Lord made away.

Womening Empowering Book means that the strength to pull down strong holds.

1. Can I see the really the real me in God word.
2. Words look powerfully than we look.
3. The Scripture the word of God help me to help other.

Women's are like the Flower of the light in a woman life this is the day of the lord we shall be rejoices and, be exceed glad. Making a Joyfully Nosie unto the Lord. This is a good day for you to talk to the Lord about how you feel about me "me myself I need answers from the Lord. And, how people can make a way out of no way

Listening to the word of God is time set up at for your needs how much time is set up with the Lord. My daily walk with the lord is now a stubble block to other but it's time to pray and given into that time to pray and, talk with the Lord.

God Word comes to heal and not tarry down.

Women's Empowering Fear:

The Word come from the Lord created that the Glory of God—He's right now with the Word of God, God word is for that person that want a deliverance rising over nothing keeping it real one man to another disease's. Fear has brought on the power to cast out Fear I got to stop Sin Death Lay aside the hurt heart at the door. Place the bad influence "thinking that you can do it without God help making the word come to pass on your on will not see what God has for you.

This Story state's that God has already created a mind of God with in you that make you feel that you are some body without hurting from the devil hurts' and, plan.

This Book has answerer you question for the next day and, the next day. Be Bless

PROPHETESS: SHARON WIMBUSH AND, FAMILY JAMAR E USCANGA" ANGELO T USCANGA.   Dedicate to my Nephews and, Niece

www.ingramcontent.com/pod-product-compliance
Lightning Source LLC
Chambersburg PA
CBHW040318010626
45792CB00023B/1007